D1316331

This is my book.

Presented to _____

by _____

on _____

First Book of
Bible Stories

CATHOLIC EDITION

Illustrated by
Lisa S. Reed
Kelly R. Pulley

Regina Press
New York

THE REGINA PRESS
10 Hub Drive
Melville, NY 11747

International Standard Book Number: 0-88271-563-1

Don Wise, Producer
Randy White, Production Manager
Performance Unlimited, Inc.
1710 General George Patton Drive, Suite 110
Brentwood, Tennessee 37027

Foreword

This collection of Bible stories is written especially for young children. It tells in simple words all about God's love from the beginning of time. These delightful stories teach your child of God's faithfulness. As you read these stories, your child will also learn about Jesus and his teachings. You will read how Jesus and the Holy Spirit started the Church on the feast of Pentecost. And you will recognize the Holy Spirit who guides the Church today. Reading the Bible stories will bring you and your child closer to God.

Before you begin, say the prayer on the following page for understanding and grace.

Prayer

Heavenly Father, grant me special grace to understand the message you have placed here for me. Thank you for always being faithful to your people—from the creation of the world up to today. May I learn from the example of your Son, Jesus, and may I grow daily in my love for you. Amen.

Introduction

The Bible has two parts, the Old Testament and the New Testament. The writers were inspired and guided by God. That is why we say the Bible is the word of God.

The Bible tells how God made the world and every living thing and how his Son, Jesus, came to us to show us the way to heaven. It is the most important story in all the world.

Table Of Contents

Old Testament

Creation	13
Adam and Eve	15
Noah and the Ark	17
Abraham and Sarah	19
Joseph and His Brothers	21
Baby Moses	23
Joshua	25
Gideon	27
Ruth and Naomi	29
Hannah	31
Samuel	33
David and Goliath	35
Solomon	37
Elijah	39
Josiah	41
Esther	43
Daniel	45
Jonah	47

Table Of Contents

New Testament

Mary and Joseph	53
Jesus at the Temple	55
John the Baptist	57
Calling the Disciples	59
The Wedding Miracle	61
Sowing Seeds	63
The Good Samaritan	65
Feeding the 5,000	67
Jesus Walks on Water	69
The Lost Sheep	71
The Prodigal Son	73
Jesus and the Children	75
Zacchaeus	77
The Last Supper	79
Jesus Is Alive	81
Peter Fills His Net	83
Jesus Goes to Heaven	85
Saul Becomes Paul	87
Jesus Will Come Again	89
The Catholic Church	91

The Old Testament

The first part of the Bible tells the story of Creation, the beginning of the world, and the first people. There are also many stories about the people God chose to bring us his message and to lead us.

All of this happened a very long time ago. No one knows exactly when because there were no such things as dates or calendars. Everything took place before Jesus was born.

Old Testament

Creation

God made the heavens and the earth. He saw the earth was dark and empty. God said, "Let there be light." He called the light "day," and the darkness he called "night."

God made a big space around the earth where he put blue skies and fluffy white clouds. God made the oceans, rivers, and seas. And he made the dry lands appear. God put beautiful flowers and trees all over the earth.

"Let there be bright lights," said God as he made the moon and stars for the night and the sun for the day. Then God filled the waters with all kinds of fish. He filled the sky with birds of all shapes and colors. God was pleased with what he created.

God covered the dry land with all kinds of animals. Then God made man and woman. He named the man Adam.

God made these things in only six days. He was pleased with all that he created. And on the seventh day, God saw that his work was done, and he rested. God blessed this day and made it holy.

Genesis 1

Adam and Eve

God made a helper for Adam. Her name was Eve. They lived in the Garden of Eden. Adam and Eve were responsible for taking care of the garden. There was a special tree in the middle of the garden. God said, "You may eat the fruit from any tree except this one."

One day a serpent told Eve, "The fruit of this tree will make you wise like God." Eve took a bite. Then, she gave some to Adam.

Later that night, God was walking through the garden. "Where are you?" asked God. "We are over here," said Adam. "Why are you hiding?" asked God. "I ate fruit from the forbidden tree," said Adam. "Eve gave it to me."

God asked Eve, "What have you done?" Eve replied, "The serpent tricked me and said the fruit would make us wise like you."

God said to the serpent, "For the rest of your days, you will slither on your belly." Then God made clothes for Adam and Eve, and they left the garden. He sent an angel with a flaming sword to guard the entrance. No one could enter the garden again.

Genesis 2-3

Noah and the Ark

God loved Noah very much. One day, God said, "I am going to wash away all the evil in the world. I want you to build a special boat called an ark."

When the ark was complete, God told Noah to put two of each kind of animal on the ark. Noah thought, "Where will I find all of those animals?" Then a great thing happened. God sent the animals to Noah.

Noah and his family loaded the ark with plenty of food. Then God said, "It is time for you, your family, and all the animals to get on the ark." After they were all inside, the hand of God shut the door.

God made it rain for forty days and forty nights. Noah and his family waited patiently for the storm to end. Finally, the rain stopped. The ark came to rest on a mountaintop. After the water went down, they all came out of the ark and gave thanks to God for keeping them safe.

God placed a rainbow across the sky. He said, "This will be a sign of my promise to all of you. I will never again cover the whole earth with water."

Genesis 6-8

Abraham and Sarah

God told Abraham to take his wife Sarah and travel to a new land. Even though they did not know where they were going, Abraham and Sarah obeyed God. They packed up their things and began their long journey. Abraham's nephew, Lot, traveled with them.

God guided them to Canaan. Abraham knew there was not enough grass and water to support two families and their animals. He said to Lot, "Choose the land you want, and go live there." Lot picked the best land for himself. Abraham and Sarah moved their tents to the big trees at Hebron.

One day, Abraham met three travelers. One of the travelers said, "Your wife will have a baby boy." Sarah laughed. She thought she was too old to have a baby.

The visitor asked, "Why did you laugh? Is there anything that God cannot do?"

When Abraham heard the visitor say this, he knew it was God speaking. Before the year was over, Sarah and Abraham had a son. They named him Isaac, which means laughter. And they gave thanks to God.

Genesis 12-21

Joseph and His Brothers

There was a man named Jacob who had twelve sons. Jacob loved all his sons, but he loved his son Joseph most of all. Jacob gave Joseph a beautiful coat with many colors. Joseph's brothers were jealous.

One night, Joseph dreamed he and his brothers were gathering grain. Suddenly, Joseph's grain stood straight and tall. The grain his brothers were gathering bowed to Joseph's grain. Joseph told his family about his dream. His brothers said, "Who do you think you are that we would bow to you?"

One day, Joseph visited his brothers as they tended sheep. When they saw him, they grabbed him and threw him in a dry well. Later, they pulled Joseph out of the well and sold him to some travelers who paid twenty pieces of silver for him.

When Joseph did not return home that night, his father was so sad he cried. He thought Joseph was dead. But Joseph was alive. The traders took him far away to Egypt where he became a slave. Later, with God's help, Joseph became a great ruler for an Egyptian Pharaoh.

Genesis 37

Baby Moses

The king of Egypt was afraid of God's people. He thought they might try to take over his kingdom. The king made God's people slaves. He made them work hard so they would be tired. One day the king shouted, "I do not like these people. Throw their baby boys into the river."

One mother prayed to God to save her baby. She hid him in a basket and floated it in the river. Then she told the baby's sister to watch over him. The king's daughter found the baby. She decided to keep him. The baby's sister asked, "Do you need someone to take care of the baby?" When the princess said yes, the baby's sister brought her own mother to help. The mother gave thanks to God.

The baby's mother got to take care of him. She taught him many things. When it came time, she took the child to live in the palace with the princess. The princess named the baby Moses. When Moses grew up, he became a great leader for God's people.

Exodus 1-2

Joshua

It was time for a new leader for God's people. Joshua was God's choice. He would be the one to lead God's people into the land God promised them. Joshua knew they needed to conquer the great walled city of Jericho before they could live in Canaan.

Joshua sent two spies to Jericho. The spies told Joshua that the people of Jericho were afraid of their God. Joshua knew this was good news. As Joshua and his men approached the city, they saw someone with a sword standing in front of them. He asked, "Are you for or against us?"

The person said, "Neither. I am for God's army." Joshua knew this was an angel sent from God. He listened carefully to the angel's instructions.

Joshua followed the angel's instructions carefully. His soldiers did not talk as they marched around the wall once each day for six days. On the seventh day, they marched around seven times. As Joshua gave the signal, the priests blew their trumpets and the soldiers shouted. Suddenly Jericho's walls fell down. Joshua followed God's instructions, and he won the battle.

Joshua 1-6

Gideon

God's people lived in the land of Canaan. Because it was such a nice place to live, a group of people called the Midianites wanted to take over the land. One day, God sent an angel to deliver a message to a man named Gideon. The angel said, "God has chosen you to be the leader of his people."

Gideon did not think he was the right person to lead God's people. So, he asked God for a sign. "Make this wool wet and the ground dry," said Gideon.

God did as Gideon asked. But Gideon said, "If I am the one to save your people, make the wool dry and the ground wet."

Again God made these things happen. So, Gideon put a big army together. God said, "The army is too big. The people must know that I made this victory possible."

God chose only three hundred men to fight the Midianites. That night the men brought only a torch, a jar, and a trumpet. When Gideon gave the signal, they blew their trumpets and smashed their jars. The Midianites ran away in fear. With God's help Gideon won the battle!

Judges 6-7

Ruth and Naomi

There was once a woman named Naomi. She and her husband had two sons. They lived in Moab. One day Naomi's husband died. Then her sons died, too. One of her sons was married to a woman named Ruth. Ruth also lived in Moab. Now they were both alone.

Naomi decided to return to the land where she grew up. Ruth said, "I will not leave you. Where you go, I will go. Your God will be my God."

Naomi realized that Ruth was determined to go with her. So Ruth and Naomi set out for the town of Bethlehem.

It was harvest time in Bethlehem when they arrived. Ruth went to gather some grain. Boaz, the man who owned the grain, asked who she was. "Her name is Ruth. She lives with Naomi," said the workers. They also told him how hard Ruth worked.

From that day on, Boaz cared for Ruth. He thought she was very kind for taking care of Naomi. Later, Ruth and Boaz got married. They had a son and named him Obed. And God blessed all of them.

Ruth 1-4

Hannah

Hannah was married to a good man. Even though he loved her, she was very sad. More than anything in the world, Hannah wanted to have a baby.

Each year, Hannah and her husband made a special trip to the temple. One day, a woman made fun of Hannah for not having children. This made Hannah so unhappy that she cried while she prayed. Hannah promised God that if he gave her a baby boy, the child would live at the temple and serve him. Hannah kept repeating her prayer over and over again.

A priest named Eli asked Hannah if she needed help. Hannah told Eli that she was praying to God for a baby.

Eli said, "You may go home in peace, Hannah. May God hear your prayers and bless you with a son."

God heard Hannah's prayers. The next year, God gave her a baby boy! Hannah named the baby Samuel, which means, "I asked God for him."

1 Samuel 1-2

Samuel

When Samuel was a young boy, he went to live at the temple with a priest named Eli. There he learned to love God and respect his word. One night after Samuel had gone to sleep, he was awakened by a voice calling him. Samuel ran to Eli's room. "Here I am," said Samuel.

Eli said to young Samuel, "I did not call you. Go back to bed."

Samuel returned to bed. Again, the voice called out to him and he ran to Eli's room. Soon, Eli realized it was God calling Samuel. He said, "When the voice calls, say 'Speak to me God, your servant is listening'."

Samuel returned to bed. He heard the voice again. Samuel did as Eli said. Then, God spoke to Samuel. The boy listened carefully. The next morning Samuel was afraid to tell Eli what God said.

"Do not be afraid to tell me what God said to you," said Eli. So Samuel told Eli everything. Now Eli knew Samuel was a prophet of God. God continued to give messages to his people through Samuel.

1 Samuel 3

David and Goliath

David was a shepherd boy who lived with his father, Jesse. One day, an enemy army came to take over the land. Saul, the king of the land, called together his own army. Three of David's brothers joined. But David was too young to fight.

Jesse sent David to take food to his brothers. As David approached King Saul's camp, he heard the king's men shout, "Look! The enemy is approaching! It is the giant, Goliath!"

The giant roared, "I will fight any of you. If you beat me, we will be your slaves. But if I beat you, you will be our slaves!"

King Saul's men shook with fear. But David told them he would fight the giant. The soldiers told the king what David said. The king called for David. He said, "You will need my sword and armor to protect you."

"Your armor is too heavy. I must fight the giant my own way. God will protect me," said David. He swung his sling, and he let the stone fly. Goliath fell down. David thanked God for giving him the courage to fight the giant and win.

1 Samuel 16-17

Solomon

When King David was very old, he called his son, Solomon, to his bedside. He said, "Soon it will be time for me to leave this earth. God will bless you, but you must promise to obey God's law."

A short time later, Solomon became king. And he followed his father's advice. God was pleased with him. One night, God came to Solomon in a dream. "Solomon," God said, "What can I give you?"

Solomon said, "Please give me wisdom to know right from wrong so that I can help your people."

God was pleased with Solomon's request. He said, "You will be the wisest and most powerful king on earth as long as you live."

Solomon's dream came true. God gave him wisdom. He ruled God's people with such great wisdom that people from all over came to hear him speak. God also gave Solomon riches. King Solomon never forgot what his father told him. He always asked God for help. And as long as Solomon followed God's law, he was blessed.

1 Kings 1-4

Elijah

E lijah was a prophet of God. A prophet tells people God's word.

God chose Elijah to deliver a message to a bad king named Ahab. King Ahab did not listen to God. This made God sad. God told Elijah to go see King Ahab.

King Ahab did not like Elijah, but he listened as Elijah said, "Because you have forgotten what is right, God has decided there will be no rain or dew for a very long time. Then you will know he is the one true God."

And just as God promised, there was no rain or dew for a very long time. But God took care of his prophet Elijah. He told Elijah to go to a brook where he would find water to drink.

Then God said, "Do not worry. I will send birds to bring you food each day." Elijah listened and did exactly as God told him. He found the brook just as God said. Each morning and evening the birds brought him food to eat. God took good care of Elijah.

1 Kings 16-17

Josiah

Many kings did not obey God and his laws. There were some kings who worshiped the sun, and others worshiped the stars. Over time they tried to destroy all the written copies of the Book of Law. The Book of Law contained the rules God gave his people.

One day a new king came into power. His name was Josiah, and he was only eight years old. As Josiah grew older, he became a good ruler for his people. He loved God.

When Josiah was twenty-six years old, he made repairs to the temple where people went to pray. A priest working at the temple discovered a copy of the Book of Law.

King Josiah told his officers to take the Book of Law to a wise woman. After reading the Book of Law, she said, "God is unhappy with the kings who worship idols. But God is pleased that Josiah wants to do what is right and follow his rules."

Josiah told the people to obey God's law. So God blessed Josiah and his people as long as he was king.

2 Kings 22-23

Esther

A beautiful woman named Esther lived with her cousin Mordecai. He taught her to love God. One day, a great ruler named King Xerxes met Esther. He liked her so much he made her his queen.

The king gave a man named Haman an important job in his kingdom. To honor Haman, the king made a law that said whenever Haman passed by, everyone must bow. Mordecai would not bow. Haman said, "King Xerxes, some of the people do not obey your laws. You must get rid of them." The king agreed.

When Esther heard of Haman's plan, she went to see the king. She said, "I would like you and Haman to dine with me today." The king accepted Esther's invitation.

At dinner, the king said, "Esther, ask me for anything. I will gladly give it to you."

Esther said, "If you love me, do not harm my people." Then she told the king of Haman's plan. The king was so angry he had Haman taken away. He told the people they would not be harmed. Esther was very brave. She had saved her people!

Esther 2-7

Daniel

There was a good man named Daniel who worked for a king. The king decided to put Daniel in charge of his kingdom. Only the king would be more powerful than Daniel. When some of the other rulers heard about the king's decision, they were jealous. They wanted to get rid of Daniel.

The rulers knew Daniel prayed to God three times each day. So they went to the king and said, "We have a new law for you. It says no one can pray to any other man or God but you. Anyone who disobeys this law must be thrown into the lions' den."

After the king signed the law, the rulers ran to Daniel's house. They watched Daniel say his prayers. Then they ran and told the king. When the king heard Daniel had broken his law, he had him thrown into the lions' den.

The next morning, the king ran to see if Daniel was still alive. Daniel shouted. "I am alive! God sent an angel to protect me." The king knew Daniel's faith in God saved him. From that day forward he and his people worshiped Daniel's God.

Daniel 6

Jonah

Jonah was a prophet. He gave messages to people from God. God told Jonah to go to the city of Nineveh and tell the people to stop doing bad things.

Jonah did not want to go. So he got on a ship that would take him far away from Nineveh. This made God angry, so he sent a great storm. The ship's captain said to Jonah, "You must call on your God. Maybe he will protect us from the storm."

Jonah said, "God is angry with me. If you throw me overboard, the storm will stop."

The sailors threw Jonah into the sea. Suddenly the storm stopped. God saved Jonah by sending a big fish to swallow him.

For three days and three nights, Jonah prayed for forgiveness and help. God heard his prayers. He told the fish to spit Jonah out onto dry land.

This time, Jonah obeyed God. He went to Nineveh. He told the people there to stop being bad. The king and his people believed Jonah's message. They began to obey God's law. This made God very happy.

Jonah 1-3

Personal Record

Name _____
   born _____ in _____

Baptism
   Date _____
   Priest _____
   Parish _____
   Godfather _____
   Godmother _____

First Communion
   Date _____
   Priest _____
   Parish _____

Confirmation
   Date _____
   Bishop _____
   Parish _____
   Sponsor _____
   Confirmation name _____

Family Record

Father _____
    born _____ in _____

Mother _____
    born _____ in _____

Brothers and Sisters _____
_____
_____

Father's Family
    Grandfather _____
        born _____
    Grandmother _____
        born _____

Mother's Family
    Grandfather _____
        born _____
    Grandmother _____
        born _____

The New Testament

The second part of the Bible is the story of Jesus, the Son of God, and his birth, life, death and resurrection.

Everything Jesus did and all the truths he taught were so important that our biggest celebrations are now related to events in his life. For example, on Christmas Day we celebrate the birth of Jesus, and on Easter Sunday we celebrate his rising from the dead.

Now that Jesus is in heaven, he continues to help us by sending the Holy Spirit to fill our hearts with love and wisdom.

New
Testamen

Mary and Joseph

A young woman named Mary was engaged to Joseph, a carpenter. One day, God sent his angel Gabriel to Mary. Gabriel said, "Do not be afraid. You have been chosen to have God's Son. You will name him Jesus." Mary was still afraid. "You must trust God. All things are possible with him," said Gabriel.

"I love God. I will do whatever he says," said Mary. Then the angel left.

After Gabriel visited Mary, an angel came to Joseph in a dream. The angel said, "Do not be afraid to take Mary as your wife. God has given her a child." Joseph listened to the angel, and he took Mary as his wife.

Mary and Joseph traveled to Bethlehem. When they arrived, all the inns were full. So that night they stayed in a stable. Mary gave birth to a baby boy. He was God's Son. They named him Jesus.

God placed a bright star in the sky above the city. The star pointed to the place where baby Jesus lay sleeping.

Luke 1-2

Jesus at the Temple

Jesus grew up in the town of Nazareth. When Jesus was twelve years old, his family went to the temple in Jerusalem. After their visit, they started their trip home. But Jesus stayed behind. When Mary and Joseph realized that Jesus was not with them, they began searching for him. For three days they looked and looked. But they could not find Jesus anywhere.

Mary and Joseph went back to the temple. There they found Jesus. He was talking with the teachers. The teachers were truly amazed! This little boy understood new and wonderful things about God. Mary was happy to see Jesus again.

Mary said, "Jesus, we have been looking everywhere for you. We were worried about you."

"Why were you looking for me, Mother? Did you not know I would be at my Father's house?" replied Jesus.

Mary did not understand, but she was glad that Jesus was safe. Then Mary, Joseph, and Jesus returned to Nazareth.

Luke 2

John the Baptist

John the Baptist loved God very much. He lived in the desert. He wore camel's hair and a leather belt. And for food, he ate locusts and wild honey.

John spent his days telling others that God would send someone special to them. Many people listened to John. They tried to obey God's rules. John took these people to the Jordan River and baptized them. He did this by dipping them in the water. This baptism showed that they loved God. As John did this, he said, "I baptize you with water. Someone else is coming who will baptize you with God's Spirit."

One day Jesus came to the Jordan River. "John, I want you to baptize me," said Jesus.

John said, "You are God's Son. It would be better if you baptized me!"

But Jesus said, "I must do what is right." So John baptized Jesus. After Jesus was baptized, God's Spirit appeared in the form of a dove. It came down from heaven and landed on Jesus. Then God's voice from heaven was heard. He said, "You are my Son. I love you. I am pleased with you."

Matthew 3

Calling the Disciples

One day, Jesus went to the Sea of Galilee to speak. He saw two boats on the beach. One of the boats belonged to a fisherman named Peter. Jesus stepped into the boat and asked Peter to push it into the water. Peter did as he was asked.

After Jesus finished speaking, he said to Peter and another fisherman named Andrew, "Row out deeper into the sea. Then throw your nets into the water. And you will catch fish."

Peter and Andrew did as they were told. When they pulled their nets up from the water, the nets were full. Peter fell to his knees and said, "Go away! You should not be seen with me. I have done bad things."

"Do not be afraid. From now on you will be a fisher of men," said Jesus. There were twelve men Jesus chose to help him. Their names were Peter, Andrew, James, John, Philip, Bartholomew, Matthew, Thomas, Thaddaeus, Simon, another helper named James, and Judas. Jesus called these twelve men his disciples. They would travel with him as he taught about God's love.

Luke 5-6

The Wedding Miracle

One day, Jesus and his disciples went to a wedding party. Mary, Jesus' mother, was also at the wedding.

Jesus' mother noticed that there was no more wine. "Jesus," Mary said, "the wine is gone, and the party is not over."

Then Mary said to the servants, "Jesus will tell you what needs to be done."

Jesus told the servants to fill six jars with water. After the servants filled the jars, Jesus said, "Now fill a cup and give it to the servant who is in charge and ask him to drink the wine." Again, the servers did as Jesus asked.

When the servant in charge took a drink, he was very surprised! "This is the best wine I have ever tasted," he exclaimed. The servants who had filled the jars with water were amazed. Jesus had turned the water into wine! This was his first miracle.

John 2

Sowing Seeds

Everyone loved listening to the stories Jesus told. One day Jesus told the people this story.

There was a farmer planting seeds in his field. Some seeds fell into the hard path and the birds ate these seeds. Some seeds fell beside the path in the rocks. The plants began to grow. But the hot sun wilted them.

Some seeds fell where there were weeds. These seeds grew, but the weeds were stronger.

But other seeds fell into the good dirt. When the seeds sprouted, it was easy for their roots to push down into the soft dirt. Soon the seeds became strong plants. As Jesus finished the story some of the people asked, "Jesus, can you please explain this story to us?"

Jesus said, "God's word is like the seeds. Some people hear it but do not take it into their hearts. Other people are like the seeds planted in the good soil. When God's love is planted in them, it begins to grow. Then they can share his love with others."

Matthew 13

The Good Samaritan

One day, Jesus told the story of a man who was traveling from Jerusalem to Jericho. As the man walked along the road, he was attacked by some robbers.

The robbers left the hurt man on the side of the road. A priest from Jerusalem saw the hurt man. He crossed to the other side of the road and continued on his way. A little while later, another man passed by the hurt man without stopping to help.

Finally a man from Samaria approached the hurt man. When he saw the hurt man, he felt sorry for him. The Samaritan went over to the hurt man. He helped the hurt man by cleaning his wounds. Then he took him to an inn. He watched over the hurt man all night.

After Jesus finished telling the story, he asked, "Which one of the three men was the good neighbor?"

Someone said, "The one who helped the hurt man."

Jesus said, "That is right! You should always help people who are in need."

Luke 10

Feeding the 5,000

One day five thousand people came to see Jesus. There were many sick and hurt people who had come to be healed by Jesus. Jesus saw how badly they needed him. Even though he was very tired, Jesus stayed until they were all healed. As he healed the people, he told them about God's love.

As it began to get dark, the disciples said, "We must send these people home."

But Jesus said, "You must feed them."

The disciples asked, "How can we feed all these people? We found a little boy who has five loaves of bread and two fish. That will not feed five thousand people."

Jesus took the fish and bread, and he thanked God for all the food. Then he broke the bread into pieces. He told the disciples to share the bread and fish with the people.

Everyone ate until they were full. Jesus had healed them, and now he had fed them. The people truly believed that Jesus was the Son of God.

Luke 9

Jesus Walks on Water

It was getting late. Jesus and his disciples had been teaching all day. "Row across the lake," Jesus told the disciples. "The crowds will not be there, and you can rest. I will come over later." The disciples got into the boat and began rowing across the lake.

As it got dark it began to storm. The disciples could not get to the other side of the lake.

The disciples saw someone coming toward the boat, and they were frightened. "Who is it?" they asked. "Who could be walking on water in the middle of a storm?"

"Do not be afraid," Jesus said. "It is I." The disciples were very surprised. What was Jesus doing out there? Jesus got into the boat.

Suddenly the wind quit blowing. The waves began to calm down. The boat stopped rocking. The disciples knew Jesus had made the storm go away. They thanked him for saving them from the storm. "You are truly God's Son," they said. "Even the wind and water obey you."

Matthew 14

The Lost Sheep

One day, Jesus heard some men talking. They said, "Why does Jesus spend time with people who do not know God?" To help them understand, Jesus told this story.

Once there was a good shepherd. He spent every day watching over his flock of one hundred sheep. Each evening, he led them back to the pen. As they entered the pen he counted them. One evening he counted ninety-nine sheep. One was lost.

The good shepherd called for the lost sheep. He looked and looked, but could not find him anywhere. Finally, he found the lost sheep. The shepherd shouted with joy. He called all his neighbors together for a party to celebrate. "My sheep was lost, but I have found him."

When Jesus finished telling this story, he said, "God loves all his children just like a shepherd loves all his sheep."

Luke 15

The Prodigal Son

Jesus told this story to a crowd of people. His story began with a man who had two sons. The older son did his chores and tried to be good. The younger son wanted to travel and see the world.

The younger son asked his father to give him some money. The father was very upset, but he gave his younger son the money. The younger son packed his things and set off to see the world.

The young man began his new life. He lived like a king. He did whatever he wanted to do. Soon all of his money was gone. He took a job feeding pigs. He was so hungry that he found himself wishing he could have some of the pigs' food.

The young man began to cry. He decided to return home and ask his father for a job. While he was still a long way off, his father saw him. They ran to each other. The father threw his arms around his younger son and said, "I thought you were lost, and now you are found. I love you, my son."

He had a big party for his son to show him how happy he was!

Luke 15

Jesus and the Children

Jesus spent much of his time talking about God and healing the sick. Jesus and the disciples were always surrounded by large groups of people. They came from far away just to see Jesus. People often brought their babies and young children with them. They wanted Jesus to bless them. And the children wanted to hear Jesus tell stories.

One day the disciples saw some children running toward Jesus. The disciples thought Jesus was much too busy to see the children. They said, "Jesus has more important things to do than visit with you." They told the parents and children to go away.

When Jesus found out what the disciples had said to the children, he was not happy. He said, "Do not stop the children from coming to see me. The kingdom of God belongs to hearts like these."

Jesus was very kind when the children came to see him. He took them in his arms and blessed them. He wanted them to know that he was not too busy for them.

Matthew 19

Zacchaeus

Zacchaeus was a short, little man who worked as a tax collector. Zacchaeus made people pay more taxes than they should have paid. He kept the extra money for himself. The people knew he took too much money, and they did not like him.

One day, Jesus and his disciples came to town. When the people heard Jesus was coming, they lined up along the streets to see him. Zacchaeus wanted to see Jesus, but he was too short so he climbed up a big tree.

Soon Jesus came walking by the tree where Zacchaeus was sitting. He looked up and said, "Zacchaeus, I am going to your house." Zacchaeus ran to his house and got ready for Jesus.

Zacchaeus told Jesus he was sorry for all the things he had done wrong. Then he gave half of what he had to the poor. And he gave back four times what he had taken from the people.

Jesus said, "Zacchaeus, I have come so people will know God. Today God is truly with you. You have listened and learned to follow God."

Luke 19

The Last Supper

Jesus and his disciples were busy preparing for a wonderful celebration called the Passover. Passover is a time when people worship God.

Jesus sent two of his disciples to prepare a room for the Passover meal. Later, Jesus and all twelve disciples gathered together in the room to celebrate. Jesus told them how to prepare the meal. The disciples did everything just as Jesus said.

Before the meal was served, Jesus brought out a bowl of water. He used the water to wash his disciples' feet.

Jesus told the disciples that the time would soon come when his life on earth would be over. When the disciples heard him say this, they were sad.

But Jesus did something very special. He took a cup of wine and some bread. He blessed it and said, "You will remember me whenever you eat this bread and drink this wine." Then Jesus and his disciples sang songs to praise God.

Matthew 26

Jesus Is Alive

After the last supper, Jesus was brought in front of an angry group of temple leaders. The leaders said, "We must get rid of Jesus. He says he is the Son of God and this is against the law." So, the temple leaders hung Jesus on a cross to die.

After Jesus died, a man named Joseph took Jesus' body and placed it in a small cave called a tomb. A big stone was used to cover the opening of the tomb. The temple leaders made some guards stand in front of the tomb to keep watch.

Three days later, an earthquake shook the ground. It made the guards fall over. An angel rolled the stone away from the tomb. This frightened the guards, and they ran away. Jesus' body was gone!

Mary Magdalene, one of Jesus' friends, was on her way to the tomb. When she saw the tomb was open, she ran inside. "Where is Jesus?" she cried.

"Do not be afraid," an angel said. "Jesus is not here. You must tell the disciples that Jesus is alive!" So Mary ran to find the disciples to tell them the good news!

Matthew 27-28

Peter Fills His Net

Mary told the disciples the good news about Jesus. They were happy. But where was Jesus? Peter wanted to see Jesus.

The disciples decided to go to the Sea of Galilee. It was dark when they arrived, and they had not eaten. So, they decided to go fishing. The disciples rowed their boat away from the shore and cast their net into the water. They fished all night, but they did not catch a single fish. Suddenly a voice called to them, "Have you caught any fish?"

"No, we have not," answered Peter.

"Cast your net out on the other side of the boat," said the voice from the shore. The disciples did as they were told. And soon their net was full of fish.

One of the disciples said, "Look! The man on the shore is Jesus!"

Peter looked up. It was Jesus! He jumped into the water and swam as fast as he could. When Peter reached the shore, Jesus was cooking breakfast. They were all happy to see him again. Now they knew Jesus was alive, and he was God's Son.

John 21

Jesus Goes to Heaven

One day, Jesus appeared to his disciples as they were eating. He said to them, "You must remember all the things I have taught you. I want you to teach them to others. Do not forget about me and the things I have taught you."

Jesus led his disciples to a place called Bethany. Jesus told them to stay in Jerusalem until they received a special gift from God.

Then Jesus lifted up his hands and blessed them. The disciples watched as Jesus went up into a cloud. The disciples waited and waited for him to come back. They wondered if Jesus had gone to heaven.

Suddenly two men wearing white robes stood beside them. The men said, "Why are you still standing here looking at the sky? Jesus has gone to heaven. One day he will come back the same way he left."

The disciples said a prayer. They gave thanks to God and praised him for all they had seen and heard.

Matthew 28; Acts 1

Saul Becomes Paul

There was a bad man named Saul. He did not believe in Jesus. He wanted to put anyone who followed Jesus into jail. Saul and some of his friends decided to travel to the city of Damascus.

As they came closer to Damascus, a bright light surrounded them. Saul fell to the ground and covered his eyes to protect them from the light. He heard a voice say, "Saul, why are you doing this to me?"

Saul was afraid. He asked, "Who are you?"

"I am Jesus, the one you do not believe in. Go into the city. There you will be told what to do," said Jesus. Saul stood up, but he could not see. His friends took his hands and led him into Damascus.

Jesus sent one of his disciples to the house where Saul was staying. The disciple put his hands on Saul's eyes and said, "Jesus sent me here to help you see again."

When he removed his hands, Saul could see. He was filled with God's Spirit. He changed his name to Paul. Paul would spend the rest of his life teaching others about Jesus.

Acts 9

Jesus Will Come Again

John was one of Jesus' closest followers and friends. After Jesus went to heaven, John taught many people about Jesus. Some leaders sent John away to live on an island. Now John would not be able to tell people about Jesus.

One day while John was praying, he heard a loud voice behind him. The voice said, "I am going to show you things that will happen in the future. I want you to write down what I show you."

John turned around and saw someone. It looked like Jesus. His face was shining brightly, like the sun. He wore a white robe and a sash of gold. John was surprised. The voice said, "I am Jesus. I was dead, but now I am alive, and I will live forever."

John saw and heard many things that day. He heard Jesus say, "I am making everything new. There will be a new heaven and a new earth. There will be no more dying and no more pain. To all those who are thirsty, I will give them the water of life. I am coming soon. I will bring your rewards with me. I am coming soon!"

Revelation 1-22

The Catholic Church

The day that Jesus went to heaven is called Pentecost. That day, the Holy Spirit entered the hearts of his disciples. The disciples then told everyone who visited in Jerusalem all about Jesus. Thousands listened and believed. When the visitors went back to their homes, they told their friends and neighbors about Jesus. Soon, people from distant lands knew about Jesus, too.

After Jesus went to heaven, Peter led the disciples. He helped them with their problems and answered their questions. Peter was also a very good preacher. Jesus had once called him "a rock." Jesus said, "On this rock I will build my Church."

The disciples now called themselves Apostles because they preached the good news about Jesus. They traveled from city to city telling everyone they met about Jesus' miracles. They told people about his death and the miracle of his resurrection. They told about Jesus' promise of everlasting life for everyone who believed.

This was wonderful news! The people who heard and believed in Jesus were

changed! They were called Christians. All the Christians together were called The Church.

The Church became very big. More and more people became Christians. But some people did not like Christians. They ordered Christians not to pray. When Christians disobeyed, they were arrested and put in jail. But the Church just grew stronger and stronger. And today, the Church is in every country all over the world!

Do you know the difference between Church and church? Church with the big C means God's people. There is only one Church and all Christians belong to it. When we say church with a small c, we mean a building where Christians gather to worship. There are many **churches** but only one **Church**.

You are part of the Church with a big C. In the sacraments of baptism and the Eucharist, you join Christians now on earth, Christians in heaven, and Christians waiting for heaven to celebrate the good news of Jesus' life, death, and resurrection. Jesus is with you always.